★ COUNTDOWN TO SPACE ★

D0204053

CHALLENGER
America's Space Tragedy

Michael D. Cole

Series Advisor:
John E. McLeaish
Chief, Public Information Office, retired,
NASA Johnson Space Center

ENSLOW PUBLISHERS, INC.

44 Fadem Road   P.O. Box 38
Box 699   Aldershot
Springfield, N.J. 07081   Hants GU12 6BP
U.S.A.   U.K.

Library of Congress Cataloging-in-Publication Data

Cole, Michael D.
   Challenger: America's space tragedy / by Michael D. Cole.
      p. cm. — (Countdown to space)
   Includes bibliographical references and index.
   ISBN 0-89490-544-9
   1. Challenger (Spacecraft)—Accidents—Juvenile literature. 2. Space shuttles—Accidents—Juvenile literature. [1. Challenger (Spacecraft)—Accidents. 2. Space shuttles—Accidents.] I. Title. II. Series: Cole, Michael D. Countdown to space.
TL867.C65 1995
629.45'4— dc20   94-41177
                                                          CIP
                                                           AC

Printed in the U.S.A.

10 9 8 7 6 5 4 3 2 1

Illustration Credits:
National Aeronautics and Space Administration (NASA), pp. 4, 6, 8, 9, 10, 11, 13, 16, 18, 19, 20, 21, 22, 23, 24, 27, 29, 31, 33, 36, 37, 38, 39, 40.

Cover Illustration:
National Aeronautics and Space Administration (NASA) (foreground); © L. Manning/Westlight (background).

CONTENTS

The seven crewmates of the Space Shuttle Challenger *(from left to right, front row) Mike Smith, Dick Scobee, Ron McNair; (back row) Ellison Onizuka, Christa McAuliffe, Gregory Jarvis, and Judith Resnik.*

A Major Malfunction

Today was to be a glorious day for Christa McAuliffe. She and her six crewmates walked across a narrow metal bridge toward the hatch of the Space Shuttle *Challenger*. She was about to live the dream of going into space.

One of the technicians at the hatch had a gift for McAuliffe. His name was Johnny Corlew. When he was a boy he often picked apples to give to his teachers at school. He would not miss the chance to give an apple to *this* teacher.

Christa McAuliffe had been chosen by the National Aeronautics and Space Administration (NASA) as the first teacher in space. The Teacher in Space program was invented by President Ronald Reagan to help boost public interest in the space program. It was working.

Schoolchildren around the country were watching the countdown on television. McAuliffe was ready to become the first private citizen ever to fly into space.

Wearing her blue NASA flight suit, McAuliffe stepped toward the hatch. Corlew gave her the apple.

This was the logo for the Teacher in Space program, an idea invented by President Ronald Reagan.

The teacher from Concord, New Hampshire, gave him a beaming smile.

"Save it for me," McAuliffe said, "and I'll eat it when I get back."[1]

In that exciting and emotional moment, McAuliffe could not have known that she was never coming back.

Commander Dick Scobee, Pilot Mike Smith, Mission Specialists Ron McNair, Ellison Onizuka, and Judith Resnik, and Payload Specialist Gregory Jarvis would also not return.

The mission was doomed from the beginning. A dangerous design flaw in the solid rocket boosters had shown signs of trouble before.[2] Now, on the morning of January 28, 1986, the temperature at Cape Canaveral was around 32°F. Icicles a foot long hung from parts of the launchpad. It was the coldest launch day ever. Too cold for a safe launch. NASA decided to launch anyway. The upper management at NASA was not aware that the cold temperatures would cause the design flaw in the solid rocket boosters to trigger a fatal explosion.

By the time *Challenger* lifted off the pad at 11:38 A.M. It was a ticking time bomb.

To the spectators around Cape Canaveral, the launch was as beautiful and perfect as any other launch. Members of the astronauts' families were there, including McAuliffe's parents. They heard the voices of *Challenger* and Mission Control on the loudspeaker.

Challenger *lifted off from Cape Canaveral at 11:38* A.M.

"*Challenger* now heading downrange," Mission Control said. "Engines beginning to throttle down to 94 percent . . . Will throttle down to 65 percent shortly. Velocity 2,257 feet per second. Altitude 4.3 nautical miles. Three engines running normally . . . Engines throttling up. Three engines now at 104 percent."

"Go, you mother!" Pilot Mike Smith exclaimed. "There's 10,000 feet and Mach point five." They were now traveling at half the speed of sound.

"Point nine," Commander Scobee said.

"There's Mach One," said Smith. *Challenger* was now supersonic. It continued to climb toward space and the orbital speed of 17,500 miles per hour. Only one minute into the launch, the shuttle was more than

30,000 feet high and was going one and a half times the speed of sound.

"Thirty-five thousand. Going through 1.5," Smith said.

"*Challenger*, Go at throttle up," said Mission Control.

"Roger," Scobee replied, "Go at throttle up," said Mission Control.

Three seconds later, the unthinkable happened.

"Uh oh," Smith said.[3]

The *Challenger* suddenly exploded in a blaze of flame, smoke, and debris. The two solid rocket boosters soared away uncontrollably to either side of the cloud. The spectators watching the launch were not sure what they had seen. The orbiter did not emerge from the

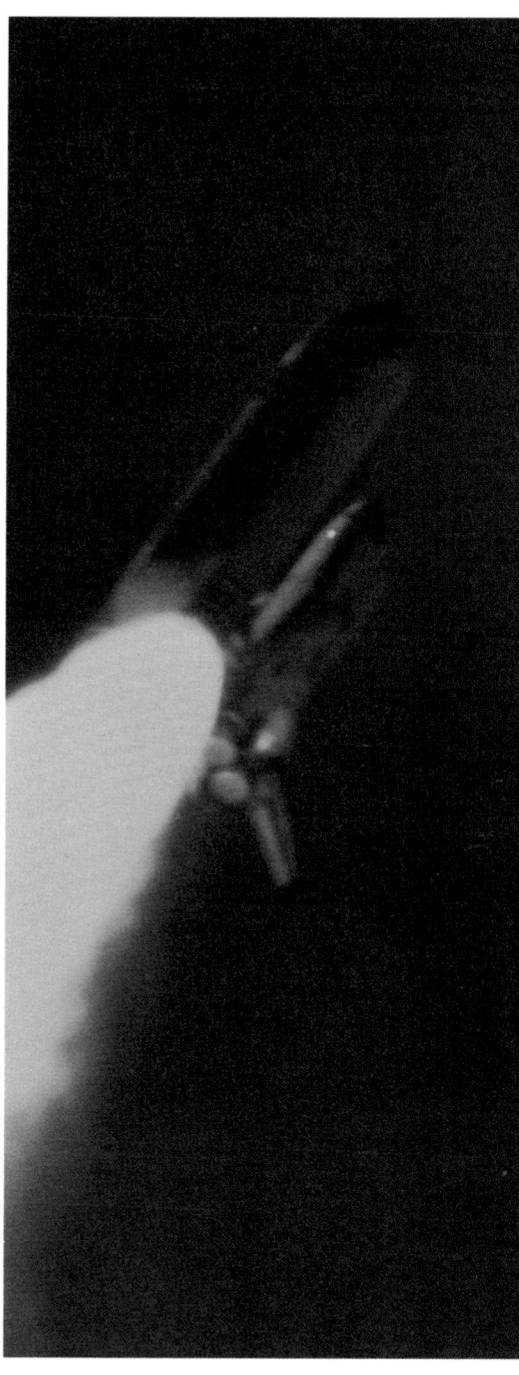

The Space Shuttle Challenger *as it begins its ill-fated climb toward space on January 28, 1986.*

cloud. The column of smoke was no longer going higher. For thirty seconds the loudspeakers were silent.

Finally the public address system announcer continued. His calm voice only added to the unreal feeling of what seemed to have happened.

"Flight controllers are looking very carefully at the situation. Obviously a major malfunction. We have no downlink." This meant there was no communication

The Space Shuttle Challenger *exploded suddenly in a blaze of smoke and debris.*

Seconds after the Challenger *explosion, an expanding ball of gas was visible from the shuttle's external tank. The worst disaster in the American space program had taken place.*

between Mission Control and the shuttle. "We have a report from the flight dynamics officer that the vehicle has exploded. The flight director confirms that. We are waiting for word of any recovery forces in the down-range field."[4]

It seemed unreal. But it was true. The *Challenger* had exploded. The worst disaster in the American space program had just taken place. And because Christa McAuliffe was aboard, it had happened before the eyes of schoolchildren around the country.

Television networks interrupted programming to

announce the tragedy. The networks followed the story with live television the rest of the day. They replayed videotape of the explosion many times, and waited for the latest news from NASA. At 4:30 P.M. NASA held a press conference. They announced that their searches of the impact area in the Atlantic Ocean showed no evidence that the crew had survived.

The crew of *Challenger* was gone. The loss of the shuttle and its crew was truly a national tragedy. President Ronald Reagan was scheduled to give his State of the Union Message to Congress that evening. He postponed the speech because of the tragedy. Instead he addressed the nation about *Challenger* later that afternoon. Some of his comments were directed at the schoolchildren who had been watching the launch.

"I know it's hard to understand that sometimes painful things like this happen," Reagan said, "It's all part of the process of exploration and discovery. It's all part of taking a chance and expanding man's horizons. The future does not belong to the fainthearted. It belongs to the brave. The *Challenger* crew was pulling us into the future and we'll continue to follow them."[5]

The story of *Challenger*'s explosion dominated the news for days after the tragedy. Reporters were told many times by many people that spaceflight is a dangerous undertaking. They were told that this sort of thing could always happen. They were told that

Americans must not give up on the space program because of this one tragedy.

As time passed, however, the story changed. The cause of the explosion was discovered in the weeks and months that followed. It became clear that the tragedy could have been avoided. The explosion of *Challenger* should never have happened.

Christa McAuliffe always took pride in the American space program. She is seen here at Kennedy Space Center.

The shuttle program was headed for disaster long before the morning of January 28, 1986. Some administrators at NASA were under political pressure to speed up the shuttle's launch schedule. "As the flight rate increased, the . . . safety, reliability, and quality assurance work force was decreasing, which adversely affected mission safety."[6] The shuttles were complex, and very difficult to repair and launch quickly.

Christa McAuliffe became an unfortunate victim of all that was wrong with NASA.

McAuliffe always took pride in the space program.[7] And throughout her training, she had taken great pride in the brief role she was going to play in it. The courage and dedication of McAuliffe and the *Challenger* crew would not be forgotten. Neither would their sacrifice. That sacrifice would begin the long journey toward a better space program and a brighter future for America in space.

Christa McAuliffe's part in that long journey began on her front doorstep.

2

Teacher in Space

One morning in August 1984, Christa McAuliffe stepped out on her front porch to get the newspaper. On the front page was the headline—REAGAN WANTS TEACHER IN SPACE.

She had heard something about the Teacher-in-Space program the day before on the radio. Now, here it was again on the front page of her hometown newspaper. Next to the story was a picture of astronaut Judith Resnik. In two days, Resnik was to become the second American woman in space. Sally Ride had become the first in 1983.

McAuliffe had no idea that in sixteen months she herself would be aboard the shuttle with Resnik. Being a teacher in space seemed like only a dream to her then. But McAuliffe would not miss a chance like this.

She read the newspaper story and saw that the only requirement was five years of teaching experience. McAuliffe had been a teacher for fifteen years. She applied. So did 11,000 other teachers around the country.

Many of the other teachers were more educated and experienced than McAuliffe. They had doctorate degrees in science or engineering. Some of them had been military pilots, or were authors of books about scientific subjects. Compared to them, McAuliffe was very *ordinary.*

She was a high school social studies teacher from Concord, New Hampshire. She was thirty-six years old, married, and the mother of two young children. With her bubbly personality and sparkling smile, she seemed like the girl next door. The key to her success as a teacher was her natural gift for communicating with young people.

After the flight, the

Astronaut Judith Resnik was the second American woman in space.

chosen teacher would spend some time as NASA's link to the public and the schools. A gift for communication would be essential. When NASA found Christa McAuliffe, they knew they had found their first teacher in space.

She intended to keep a journal of her adventure. She would teach lessons from space to schoolchildren watching the flight on television.

"I would like to humanize the Space Age," she said. "I think the students will look at that and say 'this is an ordinary person.' This ordinary person is contributing to history, and if they can make that connection then they're going to get excited about the future. They're going to get excited about space."[1]

McAuliffe trained hard for her flight. She was serious about the mission and her role as NASA's link to the public.[2] She went through weightlessness training and learned about the shuttle in simulators. True to her role as a teacher aboard the shuttle, McAuliffe prepared and practiced a pair of lessons she would teach from space. The lessons would be broadcast to about two million students across the country who attended schools equipped with satellite television receivers.

The first lesson was scheduled to be an introduction of the crew and a tour of the shuttle, including the bathroom and the galley. In the galley she would demonstrate how food was prepared. During the tour,

Christa McAuliffe trained hard for her flight. Here she undergoes weightlessness training.

McAuliffe would also point out different equipment used aboard the shuttle. The second lesson was to be a demonstration of how the production of metals, medicines, and other materials can be improved in a weightless environment.

Throughout her training, McAuliffe charmed the media. It was obvious her presence on the mission was doing a lot for NASA's image. She even made an appearance on *The Tonight Show* with Johnny Carson. By the end of the training she had gained the respect of her fellow crew members, including Judith Resnik.

Resnik, unlike McAuliffe, was uncomfortable with the public aspects of being an astronaut.[3] She was a very private, serious, and hardworking woman who had been in space before. She had a doctorate in electrical engineering, and was also a classical pianist. Resnik saw herself as a scientist, not a talk-show guest.

She accepted McAuliffe and liked her. Resnik realized a teacher in space could do a lot to communicate NASA's message. But she wondered about the wisdom of allowing such untrained people into space.

"What are we going to *do* with these people?" she once said. She did not totally object to civilians going into space. But privately she believed the missions were too expensive, too technical, and too *dangerous* to allow civilians aboard for the purposes of publicity.[4]

Resnik could more understand the presence of the other civilian on the mission, Gregory Jarvis. He was a highly trained engineer who worked for the Hughes Aircraft Company. He had helped design the Leasat satellite, which he would assist in launching from the shuttle.

Gregory Jarvis was a highly trained engineer who worked for the Hughes Aircraft Company.

Dick Scobee was the commander of the Challenger *mission.*

Still, Jarvis was not an astronaut. He was a civilian. His place on the shuttle was partly a reward to the Hughes Aircraft Company for making the shuttle the sole launching vehicle for its satellites. Jarvis's presence on the shuttle was another example of the politics at work within NASA.

McAuliffe became closest to Jarvis. They were both civilians, and led typical everyday lives in comparison to the rest of the crew. Jarvis drove a rusting 1968 Dodge Dart, spent hours riding his bicycle with his wife, and loved banana splits. He and McAuliffe played Trivial Pursuit during the slower weeks of their training. They enjoyed talking about their families and children. The two ordinary civilians worked well with the crew of professional astronauts, who were not so ordinary.

The commander of the mission was Dick Scobee. The former Air Force test pilot and father of two had been in space before, as pilot aboard *Challenger.* Scobee liked McAuliffe because they had both risen from modest backgrounds to do something special.[5] His wife was a teacher in college, so he knew something about the lives of educators.

"Shuttle missions are taken for granted these days," Scobee once told her, "but this one is unique. No matter what happens, this mission will always be remembered as the teacher-in-space mission, and you should be proud of that. *We're* all proud of it."[6]

The pilot for the mission was Mike Smith. He too was a former test pilot, but he would be making his first flight into space. Smith had never wanted to do anything but fly. As a boy he learned that the original astronauts had been test pilots. So Smith worked hard to become a test pilot after flying combat missions during the Vietnam War. Both Dick Scobee and Mike Smith were "right-stuff" astronauts in the classic mold.

Ron McNair and Ellison Onizuka represented the cultural diversity of the crew. McNair was one of the first African-American men in space. He had grown

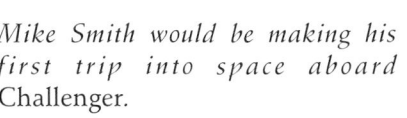

Mike Smith would be making his first trip into space aboard Challenger.

On a previous mission, Ron McNair had become one of the first African Americans to go into space.

up in a small South Carolina town and became a physicist. McNair's wife was also a teacher. His job on this flight was to operate the Spartan Halley Observatory. It would be taking photographs of Halley's comet, which was then passing near Earth.

McNair, a jazz music enthusiast, played the saxophone. On his previous mission, McNair took his saxophone with him into space. He played a few songs on it while he floated weightlessly through the shuttle. McNair would not be taking his saxophone on the *Challenger*, however—a list of other equipment took priority on this mission.

Ellison Onizuka was from Hawaii, and had been the first Japanese American in space. The former Boy Scout had wanted to become an astronaut since he was sixteen. He had been an Air Force flight test engineer before becoming an astronaut.

Onizuka also wondered about flying a teacher in space. "One should never interpret space flight as routine," he said in an interview before the launch.

"There are still a lot of questions about the Shuttle, and we need to make sure it's as safe as possible before we start flying too many civilians."[7]

The native of Hawaii hated cold weather.[8] Onizuka was the only crew member to wear a jacket to the launchpad on the cold morning of January 28. By then it was fifteen degrees warmer than it had been during the night. One of the O-ring seals on the right solid rocket booster had become brittle in the cold. It was unfit to launch.

The O-ring seals were one of the "questions about the Shuttle" Onizuka had mentioned. The solid rocket boosters dropped off midway through the shuttle launch; they were recovered from the ocean and reused. The boosters were made in sections. When the rocket was assembled, the gaps between the sections were sealed with rubber O-rings. The boosters recovered from earlier flights showed signs that hot gases had burned partway through the O-rings.

Ellison Onizuka had previously become the first Japanese American to fly into space.

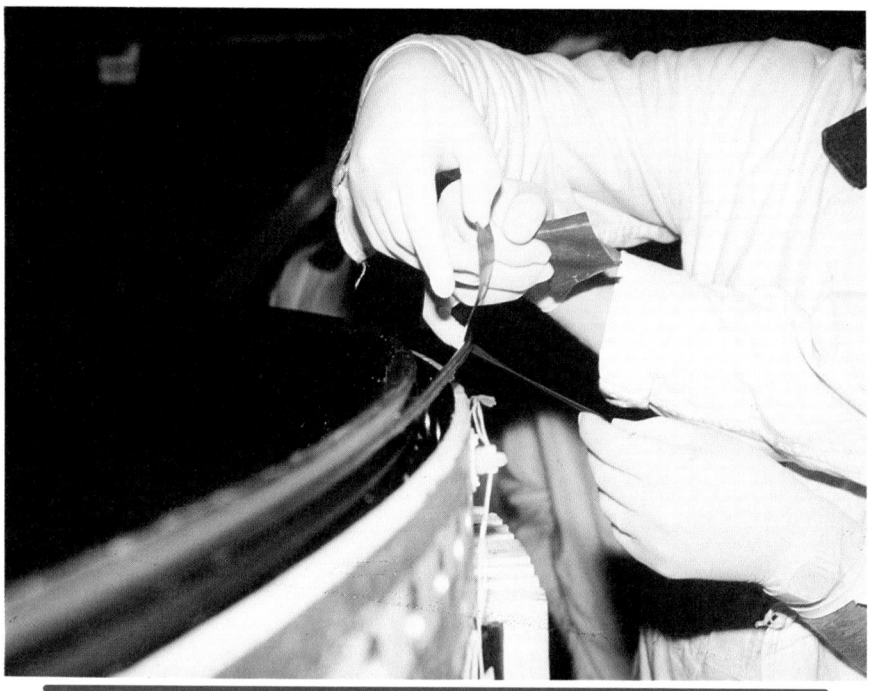

In this photo, an O-ring is studied. The safety of these O-rings was one of the questions about Challenger.

If the gases burned completely through the O-rings, it could be disastrous. Flame could escape through the gap and burn part of the shuttle or the huge external tank. If a hole was burned in the external tank, its fuel would leak. The whole assembly would explode. The crew would almost certainly be killed.

The O-ring damage had been worse when shuttles were launched in colder weather. The coldest launch so far had been 53°F. As the technician handed Christa McAuliffe the apple, it was only 32°F.

The solid rocket boosters were made by Morton

Thiokol Company. In July 1985, managers at the company had ignored a memo from one of their engineers, Roger Boisjoly. In the memo, Boisjoly warned about the O-ring problems.

"It is my honest and very real fear that if we do not take immediate action to solve the problem . . . then we stand in jeopardy of losing a flight, along with all the launchpad facilities," he wrote. "The result would be a catastrophe of the highest order—loss of human life."[9]

3

Launch and Disaster

One by one, the crew took their places aboard *Challenger*. On the flight deck were Scobee and Smith in the cockpit seats. Behind Scobee was Resnik, with Onizuka seated behind Smith. McAuliffe and Jarvis were seated side by side on the middeck below. Slightly behind McAuliffe and to her left was McNair. He was in charge of the hatch-locking mechanism.

The temperature inside the shuttle was barely 60°F.

"Cowabunga!" Resnik said of the cold.

"My nose is freezing!" Onizuka added.[1]

It was truly cold. The crew had no idea that several managers at NASA had debated throughout the night about the possible effects of the cold weather. Because of the O-rings, engineers at Morton Thiokol had again recommended against launching in the cold. But the company's managers did not want to be responsible for another delay.

The debate at NASA continued, but the concerns about the O-rings had not been passed along to upper managers of the shuttle program. So they decided to launch, unaware of the possible dangers of an O-ring failure.

An ice and frost inspection at NASA. On the day of the Challenger *launch, the weather was icy cold.*

(There was great pressure at NASA to launch the shuttle on time. Some experiments scheduled to fly on later missions would be cancelled if *Challenger* was not launched before February 1. Companies that built satellites would not want to use the shuttle if its schedule was not more dependable. NASA needed money from those companies to support the shuttle program. These were the pressures eroding the managers' attention to safety.)

The decision to launch was a faulty one. No one wanted to be blamed for a delay, so the truth about the O-rings' performance was lost somewhere in the process. And NASA unknowingly made a disastrous blunder.

On the pad, the *Challenger* crew settled in for the wait. "Good morning Christa," said a controller. He was testing the headset in her helmet. "Hope we go today."

"Good morning," she said. "Hope so too." She knew communications between launch control and the rest of the crew were vital to the countdown. So she kept quiet. Besides an occasional "loud and clear" to check her condition, these were her last known words.[2]

They again waited for hours. The launch had been cancelled the day before, after the crew had spent five hours on their backs in the shuttle.

"I hope we don't drive this down to the bitter end again today," Judith Resnik said.

Challenger, *as it was moved to its new launchpad site prior to the mission. On the morning of the launch, the astronauts waited for hours atop the launchpad.*

"Yeah," Scobee agreed.[3]

Crowds of spectators were gathering around Cape Canaveral and in the viewing stands near the launch center. In the VIP area were some members of the crew's families, including Christa McAuliffe's husband and her two young children. Her parents preferred to watch the launch from the viewing stands outside. Back at Concord High School, the auditorium was filled with cheering students. They watched on television as the countdown drew closer to the liftoff that would launch the first teacher, *their teacher*, into space.

At 11:15A.M., Scobee was told the countdown would proceed.

"All right!" he shouted. "That's great."

Resnik calculated the new liftoff time to be 11:38. Minutes later Mike Smith flipped on the switches for the auxiliary power units.

"APUs are coming on," he told Scobee.

"Got pressure in all three APUs,"Scobee said.

Challenger's own power was coming on as it disconnected from power on the ground. It was coming alive for liftoff.

"Visors are coming down," said Scobee. All crew members lowered and locked their helmet visors. As the countdown passed the two-minute mark he told the crew, "Welcome to space, guys."

The liquid oxygen vent arm retracted from the top of the external tank. They were really going this time.

"Fifteen," Scobee said as the count reached fifteen seconds. Lights blinked on the instrument panels. At six seconds the crew heard the three main engines come to life.

"There they go, guys," Scobee said.

"All right!" Resnik shouted.

"Three at a hundred," Scobee said as the three main engines reached 100 percent power. The public address system announcer counted down.

"Three, two, one, and lift-off! Lift-off of the twenty-fifth Space Shuttle mission, and it has cleared the tower."

Challenger thundered from the pad. It was a beautiful liftoff. This was the moment of glory the seven crew members, including the teacher Christa McAuliffe, had been waiting for. They were on their way to orbit.

Teachers around the country were proud that one of their own was going into space. More than two million schoolchildren watched on television as *Challenger* rocketed into the sky. It carried someone who could just as easily have been their teacher.

The Space Shuttle Challenger *lifted off on January 28, 1986. This was the moment the crew had been waiting for.*

McAuliffe wanted to make her presence aboard the shuttle something special. She wanted it to be about space, but she mostly wanted it to be about education. Her goal was to teach children new lessons from space.

In a blinding flash of flame, they were taught another lesson instead—the lesson that exploration is full of risks, including the risk of death.

Seventy-three seconds after launch, the *Challenger* exploded. The classroom celebrations around the country ended abruptly. The students watched the television closely, unsure of what they had seen. As the minutes passed the dream slowly turned into a nightmare.

They watched as the television replayed the explosion. The shuttle seemed to blow into a million pieces. It seemed unbelievable. It caused a terrible feeling inside both children and adults. A dark chill. Many of the youngsters had never had that feeling before. Their teachers had felt it maybe once or twice in their lives—when President John F. Kennedy was assassinated in 1963, or when Dr. Martin Luther King, Jr., was assassinated in 1968.

It was a feeling of shock, and loss—a deep and vivid feeling that would make the explosion of *Challenger* an unforgettable event.

Americans were in shock for days after the tragedy. Because of the media coverage of her training, the public knew about Christa McAuliffe. But they knew little about the rest of the crew. In the days that followed, they learned about Dick Scobee, Mike Smith, Ellison Onizuka, Judith Resnik, Ron McNair, and Gregory Jarvis.

America learned what a terrible loss it was.

Three days after the tragedy, a memorial service was held outside the Johnson Space Center in Houston. The large gathering included the families of the lost crew, fellow astronauts, and workers at the space center. President Ronald Reagan arrived to address the grieving families.

"The loss of your loved ones has stirred the soul of our nation," he said, "and through the pain, our hearts

After the tragedy, the public learned all about the Challenger *crew (from left to right) Christa McAuliffe, Gregory Jarvis, Judith Resnik, Dick Scobee, Ron McNair, Mike Smith, and Ellison Onizuka.*

have been opened to a profound truth: the future is not free, the story of all human progress is one of a struggle against all odds.

"We learned again that this America . . . was built by men and women like our seven star voyagers, who answered a call beyond duty, who gave more than was expected or required, and who gave it with little thought to worldly reward.

"Sometimes when we reach for the stars, we fall short. But we must pick ourselves up again and press on . . . Today we promise Dick Scobee and his crew that their dream lives on. Man will continue his conquest of space, to reach out for new goals and ever greater achievements. That is the way we shall commemorate our seven *Challenger* heroes."[4]

NASA and its astronauts would indeed press on. They believed in their work, and were committed to it now more than ever. But these were dark days for NASA.

President Reagan ordered the formation of a commission to investigate the cause of the accident. As the investigation got underway, the dark cloud over NASA grew even darker.

4

Investigation and Rebirth

The Presidential Commission on the Space Shuttle Challenger Accident was chaired by William Rogers, a former secretary of state. It was soon referred to as the Rogers commission.

Among others on the commission were Chuck Yeager, the first pilot to break the speed of sound; Sally Ride, the first American woman in space; and Neil Armstrong, the first person to walk on the moon.

The commission soon identified failure of the O-rings as the cause of the accident. Photos and videotape of the launch showed a fire plume escaping from the right solid rocket booster. The flame grew larger and eventually burned through the bottom connecting strut that held the booster to the external tank.

The bottom of the booster swung away free, while

the top of the booster swung into the tank and punctured it. Super-cooled liquid oxygen and liquid hydrogen gushed out of the punctured tank. The instant the two flammable liquids were exposed to flame, an explosion ripped the tank and the shuttle to pieces.

What most disturbed the commission and the public were the other findings.

Investigators obtained documents from NASA and Morton Thiokol about the O-rings. The commission stated that "neither Thiokol nor NASA responded adequately to internal warnings about faulty seal design."[1]

Sally Ride was the only active shuttle astronaut on the commission. She was disturbed by what she learned.

Kutyna

"I am not ready to fly again now," she told an interviewer. "I think there are very few astronauts who are ready to fly again now." She said that NASA needed to understand its own problems and fix them. Ride

William Rogers, a former secretary of state, was chairman of the Presidential Commission on the Space Shuttle Challenger Accident.

Richard P. Feyman was a member of the Rogers Commission. Feyman received the Nobel Prize in Physics in 1965.

also questioned whether private citizens were really ready to go into space.

"I think we may have been misleading people into thinking that this is a routine operation, that this is just like getting on an airliner and going across the country, and that it's that safe. It's not."[2]

It was at first believed that the crew had been killed instantly in the explosion. But study of photos showed the crew compartment had come out of the blast in one piece.

Submarines located the crew compartment in early March. It was recovered from the bottom of the Atlantic Ocean under one hundred feet of water. It was nearly intact. The bodies of all seven crew members were inside, still strapped in their seats.

Doctors worked for weeks on their remains trying to learn their cause of death. The findings were inconclusive. However, several things about their fate were learned from the wreckage.

It is certain that not all of the astronauts died from

the explosion. Four of the seven emergency air packs were recovered. Three of them had been used. More than half of the oxygen in them had been exhausted. It took the compartment two and a half minutes to fall to the water. This means that during the fall, at least three of the astronauts were breathing.

One of the packs was Mike Smith's. But his pack was mounted behind his cockpit seat. This means that it was activated by one of the other astronauts, probably Ellison Onizuka who was seated directly behind Smith.

Although at least three of them were breathing, it does not mean that they were conscious. If any part of the crew compartment was damaged or punctured by the explosion, the cabin would have depressurized. If the cabin lost air pressure at that altitude, the crew, with or without the air packs, would have lost consciousness moments later.

The crew compartment

Sally Ride was the only active shuttle astronaut on the Rogers Commission.

The U.S.S Preserver *assisted in recovery of the wreckage from the* Space Shuttle Challenger.

probably hit the water at about two hundred miles an hour. If any of them were still alive during the fall, they would not have survived the impact.

When the examinations ended, the crew's remains were flown by military transport to Dover Air Force Base in Delaware. A military honor guard carried out the flag-draped coffins one by one. Scobee and Smith were to be buried in Arlington National Cemetery in Washington, D.C. Ellison Onizuka's body was flown to Hawaii, Judith Resnik's to Ohio, Ron McNair's to South Carolina.

The remains of Gregory Jarvis were to be cremated

and his ashes scattered at sea off the coast of California. Christa McAuliffe was laid to rest near her family, friends, and former students in Concord, New Hampshire.

The long voyage of the *Challenger* crew was finally over.

Or was it?

◆　◆　◆　◆

It was late at night on the fourth of July 1988. Fifteen thousand NASA workers wore smiles as they gathered outside the Kennedy Space Center. The gleam was back in their eyes.

They were gathered in a special ceremony to watch the space shuttle *Discovery* roll out of the vehicle assembly building. Thirty months had gone by and many improvements had been made to its design. Now the space shuttle was headed back to the launchpad. It seemed like the dark days at NASA were almost over.

A section of the wreckage from Challenger *being lowered into a storage silo.*

America was ready to return to space.

Discovery was ready to launch on the morning of September 29, 1988. At 11:37 A.M., *Discovery* left the pad.

"Lift-off!" the announcer said. "Lift-off. Americans return to space as *Discovery* clears the tower."[3]

The launch went perfectly. The solid rocket boosters separated. *Discovery* thundered on toward space.

The lessons of *Challenger* were learned. The lost crew's journey and their legacy could now continue. Commander Rick Hauck said a thank-you shortly after *Discovery* entered orbit.

"We sure appreciate you all gettin' us up into orbit," Hauck said, "where we should be."[4]

Christa McAuliffe wanted *Challenger*'s voyage to be about learning. But she would be flown into space by serious, highly trained, career astronauts. As her training began, she was not sure these professionals accepted a social studies teacher from Concord, New Hampshire.

She was a little hurt one day when they asked her to leave the room before a photo session. When she was asked back in, she got a big surprise. McAuliffe found the six of them wearing short pants and short-sleeved shirts, white socks, and black graduation hats with dangling tassels. Each had an apple and a Cabbage Patch Kid lunch box. Resnik had a child's purse over her shoulder. They gave Christa a teddy bear wearing a NASA cap, and gathered around for pictures.

Christa McAuliffe laughed. Now she knew she was part of the team. She was happy. And she was very proud.[5]

Each of the astronauts knew that they had become what they were through the help of good teachers. They respected Christa McAuliffe for who she was, and they respected her profession. Together the seven of them made quite a team.

McAuliffe wanted her observations of space to truly be her own. "I want my perceptions to be honest," she said. "I want them to be just as natural as possible, and if they're very ordinary, well, that's okay."

"Maybe that's just me."[6]

The *Challenger* crew taught us an important lesson that was far from ordinary—Never stop reaching for the stars.

CHAPTER NOTES

Chapter 1

1.Robert T. Hohler, *"I Touch the Future . . ." The Story of Christa McAuliffe* (New York: Random House, 1986), p. 249.

2. *Report of the Presidential Commission on the Space Shuttle Challenger Accident*, Washington, D.C., 1986, p. 148.

3. Timothy Levi Biel, *The Challenger* (San Diego: Lucent Books, 1990), pp.39–40.

4. Richard S. Lewis, *Challenger: The Final Voyage* (New York: Columbia University Press, 1988), p. 21.

5. "From Disaster to Discovery," Great TV News Stories, ABC News Video (1989).

6. *Report of the Presidential Commission on the Space Shuttle Challenger Accident,* p. 161.

7. Hohler, pp. 26, 64–65.

Chapter 2

1. Timothy Levi Biel, *The Challenger* (San Diego: Lucent Books, 1990), p. 32.

2. Robert T. Hohler, *"I Touch the Future . . ." The Story of Christa McAuliffe* (New York: Random House, 1986), pp. 170–173.

3. Ibid., pp. 201–203.

4. Malcolm McConnell, *Challenger: A Major Malfunction* (New York: Doubleday & Company, 1987), p. 97.

5. Hohler, pp. 149–150.

6. Ibid., p. 150.

7. Ibid., p. 209.

8. McConnell, pp. 223–224.

9. *Report of the Presidential Commission on the Space Shuttle Challenger Accident,* Washington, D.C., 1986, pp. 249–250.

Chapter 3

1. Malcolm McConnell, *Challenger: A Major Malfunction* (New York: Doubleday & Company, 1987), p. 224.

2. Robert T. Hohler, *"I Touch the Future . . ." The Story of Christa McAuliffe* (New York: Random House, 1986), p. 250.

3. McConnell, pp. 230–231.

4. Timothy Levi Biel, *The Challenger* (San Diego: Lucent Books, 1990), p. 45.

Chapter 4

1. *Report of the Presidential Commission on the Space Shuttle Challenger Accident*, Washington, D.C., 1986, p. 148.

2. "From Disaster to Discovery," Great TV News Stories, ABC News Video (1989).

3. Ibid.

4. Timothy Levi Biel, *The Challenger* (San Diego: Lucent Books, 1990), p. 58.

5. Robert T. Hohler, *"I Touch the Future . . ." The Story of Christa McAuliffe* (New York: Random House, 1986), p. 164.

6. Ibid., p. 253.

GLOSSARY

auxiliary power units (APUs)—The additional or reserve electrical power sources aboard the space shuttle.

downlink—The radio communication between Mission Control and a spacecraft.

external fuel tank—The large tank filled with liquid fuel that feeds the shuttle orbiter's main engines.

O-ring—The large rubber ring used to seal sections of the solid rocket boosters together.

solid rocket booster—A rocket that uses explosive powders for fuel.

space shuttle—The reusable U.S. space transportation system that carries astronauts, satellites, and experimental scientific equipment into Earth orbit.

supersonic—Faster than the speed of sound.

FURTHER READING

Biel, Timothy Levi. *The Challenger*. San Diego: Lucent Books, 1990.

Billings, Charlene. *Christa McAuliffe: Pioneer Space Teacher*. Springfield, N.J.: Enslow Publishers, 1986.

Bond, Peter. *Heroes in Space: From Gagarin to Challenger*. New York: Basil Blackwell, Inc., 1987.

Hohler, Robert T. *"I Touch the Future..." The Story of Christa McAuliffe*. New York: Random House, 1986.

Lewis, Richard S. *Challenger: The Final Voyage*. New York: Columbia University Press, 1988.

McConnell, Malcolm. *Challenger: A Major Malfunction*. New York: Doubleday & Co., 1987.

INDEX